Table of Contents

W9-BFG-171

Driving a Big Rig

As a girl, I wanted to be a stewardess and see the world. If someone had said, "Someday you will be driving a big truck and seeing the United States and Canada from behind the wheel," I would have said, "You're not playing with a full deck."

To be honest, I didn't actually start out behind the wheel of a big rig. I began my adult life in the medical field, where I spent 25 years, working for various doctors, dentists, plastic surgeons, neuro-

Marilyn behind the wheel

surgeons, and in the pediatric operating rooms and x-ray departments of various hospitals.

In addition to my job, I was always active with my children in the Girl Scouts, Little League, the PTA and as coach for the girls softball and basketball teams and Pop Warner football with the boys.

Then in 1983, with my children in college, I decided to become a truck driver like my husband so that I could spend more time with him. He encouraged me to get my trucking license. As it turned out, I ended up driving 18-wheelers for 20 years, not retiring until 2003.

During that time I was chosen as an American Road Team Captain (1999) and as Company Driver of the Year for Truckload Carriers (2000). In addition, from 1999 to 2001, I served as a member of the National Transporation Safety Board where I acted as spokesperson for the trucking industry in matters of safety. For one year during this time I pulled a trailer whose sides were painted to show how to drive safely around big rigs. *(see page 67)*

Life in a Big Rig

For truckers the CB[1] is our lifeline. We get reports on the weather, accidents, traffic conditions, police activities, hazards on the road, or weight station activities. We learn new information on trucking changes. Sometimes it helps us locate a place of business for pick-up or deliveries.

The language we use is very simple and short – a truckers' jargon. If we are going in different directions, we have only a very few minutes to talk to one another. However, if we are going the same way, we can chat for hours. We use channel 19, or channels 15 or 17 on the West Coast. There are a lot of channels on the CB Some are fine-tuned and we can hear for miles and miles away. To identify ourselves we all have a "handle," a CB "nickname." Some we pick; some were stuck on us.   Mine is "Mrs. C."

There are locals in some towns who have CBs in their homes or autos, and who can help drivers find the location for deliveries or pick-ups and can also give them a better way to bring a 53-ft. trailer into the plant if there are hazards such as low wires, low bridges, narrow streets, trees, small turns. We really appreciate this, we do not like to back up blindsiding if we don't have to.

There have been occasions when we can assist someone in trouble on the other side of the freeway by calling for someone to help.

---

1   Citizens Band radio (CB) is, in most countries, a system of short-distance radio communiation between individuals on a selection of 40 channels within the single 27 MHz (11 meter) band.

continued on page 7

4

How'd ya know I was a truck driver?

The Good Guys

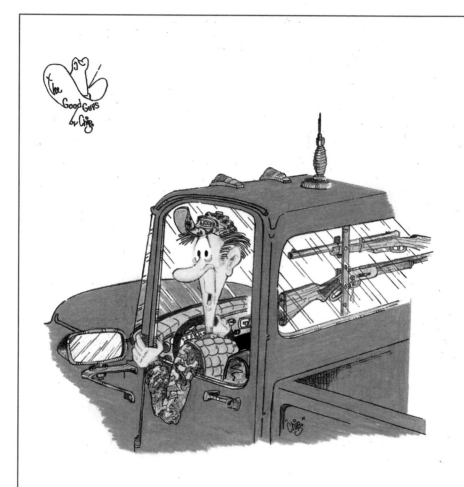

Shoot? Naw, thur not fer shootin'. Them's fer lookin' at.

continued from page 4

We can also call for a smokie (police) to help. They monitor our channel.

Trucking is a business. We are working and making a living. When the wheels don't turn, we don't make any money. We are also on a schedule and usually have a short time frame for a job. Some shippers or receivers believe the time for your appointment is etched in stone; they don't want to hear about traffic problems. Sometimes delays at one place snowball down the whole day.

One of the ways to lose a lot of time is to get hung up at a chicken coop (weigh station).   It's possible to spend hours there -- and money, too, if they find any violations.

We don't get home as often as we would like. We do without all the comforts of home and family. It can get very cold and very hot on the road. Food is not always available when we get hungry. Nor is it always easy trying to find a place to park 75 feet of truck and tractor. Bathrooms are always very difficult to locate.

The trucking industry is made up of people from all kinds of previous professions. I have met school teachers, attorneys, contractors, firemen, paramedics, police, housewives, as well as all sorts of teams: sister teams, fathers and sons, brothers, husbands and wives. We become a family, and we look after one another and help when we can.

Breaker, Breaker!

While driving down the interstate, here is some typical CB chit chat you might hear on the road.

Going east out of Shaky[1] on I-10, I hear someone holler!

R: Marilyn's Trucking, you got your ears on[2]?
M: Ya! come on back![3]
R: Is that you Mrs. C?
M: You got it.
R: It's double "R."
M: Hey, long time no hear. How've ya been?
R: Great! Ridin' and a glidin'.
M: Just came out of the yard[4], headin' for Shaky.
R: Too bad! Just left on my way to the Tar Hill[5].
M: Catch you on the re-bound, keep the shiny side up[6]. 10-4[7].

A short way from Dallas, while being passed by another truck, I holler,

M: You are clear[8], Big Red[9]!
B: Thank you ma'm. Where are you heading?
M: The Tar Hill.

---

1 Los Angeles.
2 Is your CB on?
3 Answer me.
4 Terminal, a company's place of business.
5 North Carolina.
6 Don't have an accident and roll over.
7 Bye for now.
8 You have passed me and can pull back into the lane.
9 U.S.Xpress.

continued on page 11

The Good Guys

Uh' no, Officer. I don't have one of them there "CB Lingo" books, so when you kept saying "Back it down, Stick Hauler" and "Stay off the zipper," I didn't know what you meant and I didn't know you were talking to me!

The Good Guys

No, Johnson. That's not what I meant
when I said to use a radar gun.

continued from page 8

B: I lucked out for Bean Town[10].

M: Nice looking Volvo! You get good fuel miles?

B: 5 mpg. Still new. Should improve!

M: Well, she is a beauty.

B: Thanks. Stopping at the Flyin' Hook[11] ?

M: Not this time. Well, be safe. Catch you out there. 10-4.

Pulling into the receivers yard, onto the dock with my bills, I ask manager where he wants it.

Ma: Put it into dock 6.

M: You got it.

After bumping the dock[12], I am reminded that this is a fingerprint load[13]. So, grabbing my gloves I ask how he wants it.

Ma: New pallets and 5 high.

This means drag new empty pallets into the trailer and start re-stacking the load. When I am finished, they would come in and drag it out with the fork lift. This is not my favorite chore. It usually takes 2-3 hours to unload a 53-foot trailer.

Back on the road, I'm heading for the next pick-up, and traffic is heavy. Trying to find the next shipper, I holler on my C.B.

---

10 Boston
11 A truck stop named the Flying Hook.
12 Touching the loading platform with the truck.
13 It must be unloaded by hand, usually by the driver.

Breaker, Breaker!

M: Breaker, Breaker![14] Anyone with a copy[15]?
L: You got it.
M: Is there a paper factory around here?
L: Sure, just take the next two blocks on the right and turn left.
M: Thanks.

That was a local who answered. They are great.

Pulling into the plant, after setting the brakes, I walk to the office.

M: I am here for the load to Florida.
O: OK. Back into door 3. You need to count.
M: Yes, Sir.

After loading, and rolling down the road, I think I recognize a tractor pulling a Landstar trailer.

M: Is that you, Sea Dog ?
L: You got it, Babe.
M: Mrs. C. here.
L: Well, how the heck are ya?
M: Great! You been running hard?
L: Yes. Just came from the Left Coast[16].
M: Are you empty?
L: No.
M: Where are you unloading?
L: Just ready to go in and bump the dock where you were coming out.
M: Well, I have to move on. To the Bikini State[17]. How about you?

---

14 Anyone listening?
15 Anyone listening?
16 West Coast.
17 Florida.

Breaker, Breaker!

L: I'm workin' my way across the GW[18] to the Big Apple[19].

L: Well, stay safe.

The GW Bridge leading into the Big Apple

M: you too.

After the Bikini, I'm heading west on I -10 when I'm asked,

E: Hey, West Bound, how does it look behind you?

M: East bound, you have got one coming at you[20]. 10-4.

---

18 The George Washington Bridge.
19 Manhattan.
20 Police coming toward you.

Breaker, Breaker!

Further on, JB says

JB: Marilyn's Trucking, you have a gator[21] on the zipper[22] at mile marker 101. 10-4.

M: Thanks, East Bound. Last thing was a diesel bear[23] on the ramp at 123. 10-4

JB: Where you headin'?

M: Mardi Gras[24], what is your 20[25]?

JB: 2 trucks behind you in the parking lot[26]. 10-4.

M: Well, come up here and run my front door[27].

JB: You got it. Did you see that 4-wheeler[28] going east?

M: Ya, looks like bear bait[29] to me. 10-4.

JB: Do you have another load waiting in Mardi Gras?

M: Going to drop this box[30] and pick up a set of pups[31] for Armadillo[32]. You have time to stop at the Pilot[33]?

JB: Wish I could, but I better hammer down[34].

---

21 A tire in the road.
22 Center line.
23 Police dedicated to tracking and ticketing trucks.
24 New Orleans.
25 Where are you? (Drivers don't always know who they are talking to.)
26 A car hauler.
27 Go ahead of me.
28 A passenger car.
29 A passenger car going over the speed limit.
30 A trailer.
31 Two or more trailers, usually smaller than the normal 53 feet.
32 Amarillo, Texas.
33 A truck stop.
34 Speed up.

continued on page 17

The Good Guys

Hey, Honey, what the hell is a constable?

The Good Guys

Yes. They guarantee to get to your new home with every bed bug you had at the old place!

Breaker, Breaker!

continued from page 14

M: Nice jaw jackin'[35] with ya.

After, dropping in Armadillo and picking up a new load, the weather starts getting sour. On I-40 East Bound comes on.

EB: Answer your tellie[36].
M: You got it, East Bound.
EB: You have a 10-33[37] west at the line.
M: Are they backed up?
EB: Yes. A 4-wheeler and a bull wagon[38]. 10-4
M: You look good back to Armadillo.

Later on:

M: Pony Express[39], how do you like your new Pete[40]?
P: Super. Runs real smooth.
M: She sure is beautiful!
P: Thanks.
M: I have been looking at the new K.W.[41]
P: They're great too. 10-4 .
M: Where are you heading?
P: Flag[42], to get my oil changed. I better stand on it[43].
M: I need to be in the Sticker Patch[44] sooner than I would like. 10-4.

---

35 Talking.
36 CB.
37 An accident.
38 A trailer that carries cattle, horses, pigs, etc.
39 A mail truck.
40 A Peterbuilt truck.
41 A Kentworth truck.
42 Flagstaff, Arizona.
43 Go fast.
44 Arizona.

Breaker, Breaker!

After unloading in the Sticker, it is time to call it a day. My 70 hours are up for the week. The next day, ready to roll again, I am dispatched to load and take it to Ut[45].

Rolling up through Arizona, I hear someone say a city kitty[46] is coming up behind me. After he passes (he is after a 4-wheeler), he starts his bubble gum lights[47] and gets his man.

As soon as I arrive in Ut, it starts snowing pretty heavy. This always slows you down. Now on I-15 going north, a smokie[48] comes on the C.B.

S: Marilyn's Trucking, you got a copy?
M: Yes Sir!
S: Just telling you there is a 10-33 on your front door[49]. Back it down[50]. It is going to be a long wait. 10-4
M: Thank you, Sir.

North bound in Idaho, the temp is down to 32. After fighting the black ice, I am glad to stop at the Petro in Jerome for the night. After a good night's rest, it's time to grab some breakfast and start the day. Starting the day means doing a safety check on my truck and trailer. A VI (vehicle inspection) is required by law.

---

45 Utah.
46 A local police car.
47 Flashing lights.
48 A policeman.
49 Ahead of you.
50 Slow down.

continued on page 21

Officer, I was following this shiny hiney and using it to put on my make-up, and that dummy stopped short!!!

The Good Guys

Taking a Break at the Pickle Park

Sure, tie that bull wagon up to the hitching post and grab a cup of joe while you work on your comic book. We're gonna have biscuits and gravy in a while.

continued from page 18

Then on to my paper work. Updating my comic book[51], which is also required by law.

Back on the road, the bears really have their hands full clearing the road.

M: Hey, South Bound large car. How does it look behind you?

SB: North bound, the roads are greasy[52] on Cabbage![53] 10-4.

Well, he was right. Time to hang iron[54] again. Cabbage is a very rough road even in good weather.

M: Hey, Wally World[55], I am going to squeeze in front of you. 10-4.

After driving 5 miles, stopping and taking the chains off is just as difficult. In all these years I have never gotten used to it. My fingers freeze.

On the road, after stopping in Pendleton, it's off to Portland. 4 hours later, time to fuel up and find some hot joe[56]. 3 hours up the road I head south. The chicken coops[57] are open. Usually, the pre-pass (a green light to pass the scales) is on. This time they give me the red light, so over

---

51 My log book.
52 Slippery.
53 Cabbage Mountain Highway.
54 Put on chains.
55 Walmart.
56 Coffee.
57 Weigh station.

the scales I drive. They visually check the truck and trailer, weight, lights, permits, tires, length of tractor and trailer and more.

Everything OK so on to my drop[58]. Arriving at the distribution, I set the 4 ways[59] and look for the office. Inside, the receiving office the supervisor asks me for the bills. He then tells me:

S: Ok, put it in door #12.
M: Do you want to break the seal?
S: You can break it.

The seal is put on the doors of the trailer to protect the load from vandals and ensure nothing changes from the time it is loaded at the shipper's.

After, opening the doors and backing in, I grab my gloves and head back to the office. The supervisor stops me and says,

S: You don't have to unload. We have people here that can do it.
M: O.K. I still need to count it.

Finding door 12 they are ready to drag the pallets off one by one with the fork lift. I can also tell if there is any damage to the freight that might have occurred in transit. All 1400 pieces OK, papers signed, time to leave. (Papers are the bills signed by the receiver. I need these to get paid.

---

58 Destination.
59 Warning lights.

continued on page 25

The Good Guys

You sure can tell these Owner/Operators are getting a lot younger.

The Good Guys

Breaker, breaker. Better slow that stage coach down. The grown-ups are out in force today and they just gave me a safety award.

---

continued from page 22

After updating my comic book, I find a load going east. I am always looking for a good paying load. This one pays 2.85 per mile. This is great. Usually it's hard to find freight out of here that pays this good. You take the good with the bad. It's even better with a pre-loaded trailer.

Well time to clean up and get over to load. I need to get my baby washed and clean the road scum off. There is a Streakin' Beacon[60] here. After dropping my empty and hooking up to the new trailer and doing my paper work I think I'd better scale this load. It feels heavier that the bills say. Whew, close, I will have to adjust the weight.

After moving the tandems, I am on my way.

EB: Hey, West Bound, what is happening at the scales?
M: They're spot checking, East Bound.
EB: Thanks for the come back.

As I pull across the scale, the scale master hollers on the speaker

SM: Pull it over, Marilyn's Trucking, and pull into bay #3. 10-4.

As the D.O.T. inspector waves me in, he jumps up on my running board and starts giving me instructions.

---

60 A place to get your tractor and trailer washed. The best known is a company called Blue Beacon.

DOT: Hand me your log book and bills of lading and medical card, and license. Turn on your lights first, and then the brakes. Put on your flashers, wipers. I am going to crawl under your trailer and when I say step on the brakes, hold and release.

After, all of this, he gives me back all my papers and I am released to go on my way.   But, first, I have to document the time and place of this check in my comic book. At least I received a new up-dated sticker on my windshield. This is a safety sticker that will keep me from another inspection down the road for a while. This is always stressful. You never know if they will find some problem you didn't find when you did your safety inspection. After going up and over Snoqualmie Pass, light snow falling, no chains are required yet. Just before Ellensburg I blow a tire on the trailer.

WB: East bound you O.K.? 10-4
M: I can get to the truck stop.
WB: You lost a mud flap too.
M: Thanks for the info.

Just another day on the road. These things happen when you least expect it. All and all traveling in Montana has always been a trip through God's country, even in winter. This is one reason, I really enjoy driving out here. You never see the same thing twice. Some of our country is so beautiful. After repairing the tire and putting on a new mudflap, time to get underway. This load goes to North Dakota.

The Good Guys

Breaker, Breaker, in the white KW with the pups. I'm in the skateboard on your donkey. This is my first run and picking up in the Gay Bay.

The Good Guys

Hey, Winnie. Are you watching for the County Mounty?
No ... Looking for that rice jockey.

Lingo 101

10-4 – several meanings: yes; over to you; bye for
 now

10-10 - signing off the CB

10-30 – an accident

10-36 - a driver asking the time

13'6" - maximum height of a trailer

20, WHAT'S YOUR 20? - Where are you? In traffic
 a driver does not always know who he is
 talking to.

34 hours - required layover between driving legs

4-WHEELER - a passenger car

53' - standard trailer length

5 mpg - typical diesel mileage

5th wheel - a big plate where you hook your trailer

70 hours - maximum driving hours per week

BACK IT DOWN - slow down

BARRELS - construction barrels

BEAR - a policeman in a police car

BEAR BAIT - usually a passenger car driving over
 the speed limit

Lingo 101

BED BUGGER - a furniture hauler

BETWEEN THE LINES - driving between the highway lines and not swerving to the right or left

BIG ROAD - the Interstate

BIG WORD, What's the big word? - a driver asking if the scales are open or closed in front of him

Back it down

BLUE LIGHT SPECIAL - flashing lights on police cars

BOBTAILS - tractor without a trailer

BOTTOM DUMP - a trailer that loads from the top and unloads out the bottom

BOX - trailer

BRAKE CHECK - the traffic in front of you is
slowing down or stopping

Smokie on the lookout for bear bait

BREAKER, BREAKER! - Anybody listening?

BRIDGE LAW - length between the back tires on
the tractor and back tires on the trailer

BUBBLE GUM LIGHTS - flashing lights on police
cars

BULL WAGON - a trailer that carries cattle,
horses, pigs, sheep, etc.

BUMP THE DOCK - when the trailer touches the
dock to be loaded or unloaded

Lingo 101

CAB OVER - the cab is over the engine

CASH BOX - the beginning of the turnpike or the end where you pay

CB HANDLE - a nickname a driver goes by on the CB (Mine is Mrs. C.)

CHICKEN COOP - weigh station

CHICKEN HOUSE - weigh station

CHICKEN TRUCK - a truck that carries chickens, usually a refrigerator truck

A long line of trucks waiting to enter the scales.

The chicken house on Interstate 10 in Banning, CA

CHIP TRUCK - a truck that carries chips of wood, usually a trailer with a net on top or a net on the back.

CITY KITTY - local police car

COLLAR - give someone a ticket

Crank up

COME ON BACK – Answer me.

COMIC BOOK - log book

COMING AT YA - police coming toward you

COMPANY CHANNEL - a channel on the CB that some company drivers pick to talk to one another

Lingo 101

CONSTABLE - a middle-western term to designate an officer higher in rank than a sheriff

COOL THE TIRES - take a short break by the side of the road

COOPS - weigh station

COUNTY MOUNTY – sheriff

COVERED WAGON - a flat bed trailer with portable sides and sometimes a cover

COWBOY, RUNNING LIKE A COWBOY – changing lanes frequently

CRANK UP - shift up

CROTCH ROCKET – a motorcycle

CUT THEM LOOSE - police releasing someone who's been collared

DIESEL BEAR - police in a plain colored car, dedicated to tracking, inspecting, and ticketing big trucks

DONKEY, ON YOUR DONKEY - someone coming up close behind you on your backside.

DOUBLE - a tractor with 2 trailers

DOUBLE NICKEL - 55 mph

DOUBLES - 2 trailers pulled by a tractor

DROP DECK - a flat bed trailer that is low to the
     ground

Double Nickel

DROPS - places where freight is delivered when
     a single load is divided and delivered to
     several destinations

DRY BOX - a trailer that carries dry freight

EVIL KNIEVEL - motorcycle police

FIFTH WHEEL - a big plate where you hook your
     trailer

FINGERPRINT LOAD - freight that is loaded or
     unloaded by hand, usually by the driver

FLASHING LIGHTS - a police car with its lights
     flashing

Lingo 101

FLATBED - a trailer without walls that can carry large freight, sometimes a plane or its engine

FLIP - to make a U-turn

FLYING J - a truck stop called the Flying J

FOUR-WHEELERS - passenger cars

FREIGHT HAULER- a driver hauling freight

FULL GROWN - highway patrol

FULL GROWN ROLLIN' - police on the move

GARBAGE HAULER - a truck that pulls a refrigerator trailer

GATER - a piece of tire in the road

GOING TO THE HOUSE - a driver saying he is going home

GOT A COPY - one driver asking another if he has his radio (CB) on

GOUGE ON IT - speed up

GREEN STAMP - a toll road

HAMMER DOWN - speed up

HAMMER LANE – the fast lane of the freeway

HANGIN' IRON - putting chains on your tires

HAVE YOU GOT YOUR EARS ON? - are you listening?

HAZMAT - hazardous material

HEADACHE RACK - rack behind the cab of the tractor pulling a flatbed

Hangin' iron

HOOK - a tow truck

HOURS - the hours a driver can drive

JUNK YARD - a company location which drivers report to

LIVE LOAD - freight waiting for a truck to arrive to be loaded

LOAD LOCKS - long bars a driver puts inside his trailer to keep his freight from moving

LONGHAUL - 48 states

LONG-NOSED TRACTOR - the engine sticks out in front of the cab

LOVES - a truck stop

LTL - truck that travels to another point and then directly back

MILE MARKER - a number on the side of the road that tells you where you are

MOUNTED ON THE SADDLE- two tractors hooked together, one on the 5th wheel of the first tractor

MUD FLAPS - flaps required behind all the tires

NEW RUBBER - new tire

OUT OF SERVICE - usually a driver has been put out of service at a weigh station for no more hours to drive

PARKING LOT – a car hauler

PETRO - a truck stop

PICKLE PARK - a rest area

PIGGY BACK - a tractor that carries other tractors on its saddle

A long-nosed tractor with 2 pups

PILOT - a truck stop named Pilot

PLACARDS - signs required on the truck if it is hauling hazmat. If there are bypass routes, they are required to use them. In some states they can't go in tunnels.

Lingo 101

PLAIN WRAPPER - an unmarked police car

PONY EXPRESS – a mail truck

PUPS - 2 or more trailers, usually smaller than the normal 53' trailers

A triple (3 pups)

PUTTIN' HER TO BED - shutting down the truck for the night

RADIO CHECK - a driver asking another driver if his CB was sounding O.K.

REEFER - a refrigerator trailer

RESTRICTED ROUTES - every state has roads that are limited to certain weights and lengths of trucks and trailers

RICE JOCKEY - a motorcyclist who is stretched out horizontally over the motorcycle going 90 mph

RUNNING LIKE A COWBOY – changing lanes frequently

RINGIN' YOUR BELL - someone calling you

RIPS - a truck stop called Rip Griffins

ROCK 'n' ROLL, Let's rock 'n' roll. Let's start driving.

ROCK BUCKETS - gravel haulers

A stick hauler

ROCK HAULER - a trailer that can carry heavy loads, usually rocks

ROLLIN, ACROSS - the scales are just moving the trucks across without really inspecting them.

Lingo 101

ROUND ROBIN – truck that travels to another point and then directly back

RUNNING SINGLE - someone driving alone

RUNNING LIKE A COWBOY – changing lanes frequently

A snub-nosed cab-over bobtail. Marilyn's first tractor.

RUNNING YOUR FRONT DOOR - driving a short distance in front of you

SAFETY AWARD - a ticket

SCALES - weigh station

SHOW OFF LANE - the fast lane of the freeway

SKATE BOARD - a flat bed

SMOKIE - a police officer

SNUB-NOSED TRACTOR - The cab is over the engine.

STAGE COACH - a tour bus

STAND ON IT - speed up

STICK HAULER- a trailer that carries large logs

STREAKIN' BEACON – a place to get your tractor and trailer washed. The best known is a company called Blue Beacon.

TAIL GATE - driving too close to the driver in front of you

TANKER YANKER - a tanker truck

A tanker yanker

TARP IT DOWN - a flat bed truck driver covering his load

TELLY - your CB

TERMINAL - a place of business for drivers to stop

THERMOS BOTTLE - a tanker truck

Lingo 101

TRIPLE - a tractor with 3 trailers

UNITS – tractors

WHAT'S YOUR 20? - Where are you? In traffic
a driver does not always know who he is
talking to.

YARD, BACK TO THE YARD - a driver saying he is
going back to his own company's place of
business

ZIPPER - the center line

The zipper

STATES QUIZ

Match the nicknames with the state names.
Answers on page 76.

BIG SKY	ARIZONA
BIKINI	ARKANSAS
BUCKEYE	CALIFORNIA
GARDEN STATE	FLORIDA
GRANITE STATE	MISSOURI
GREEN MOUNTAIN STATE	MONTANA
HILLBILITY	NEW HAMPSHIRE
HOG COUNTRY	NEW JERSEY
KEY STONE	NORTH CAROLINA
LEFT COAST	OHIO
MISERY	OKLAHOMA
OAKIE	PENNSYLVANIA
STICKER PATCH	UTAH
TAR HILL	VERMONT
UT	WEST VIRGINIA

Lingo 101: Cities

ARMADILLO	AMARILLO, TEXAS
ASTRO	HOUSTON, TEXAS
BEANTOWN	BOSTON, MASSACHUSETTS
BIG-A	ATLANTA, GEORGIA
BIG-D	DALLAS, TEXAS
BRIGHT LIGHTS	KANSAS CITY, MISSOURI
CACTUS PATCH	PHOENIX, ARIZONA
CHOO CHOO	CHATTANOOGA, TENNESSEE
CIGAR	TAMPA, FLORIDA
MILE HIGH	DENVER, COLORADO
FLAG	FLAGSTAFF, ARIZONA
GAY BAY	SAN FRANCISCO, CALIFORNIA
K-TOWN	KNOXVILLE, TENNESSEE
LOS WAGES	LAS VEGAS, NEVADA
MARDI GRAS	NEW ORLEANS, LOUISIANA
MUSIC CITY	NASHVILLE, TENNESSEE
RIVER CITY	MEMPHIS, TENNESSEE
SHAKY	LOS ANGELES, CALIFORNIA
SMOKE	BIRMINGHAM, ALABAMA
THE BIG APPLE	NEW YORK CITY
THE CIRCLE	INDIANAPOLIS, INDIANA
THE ROCK	LITTLE ROCK, ARKANSAS
WINDY	CHICAGO, ILLINOIS

BIG 'R' - Road Way

BIG RED - U.S. Xpress

BROWNIE - UPS

BULL DOG – Mack Truck

FED EX - Federal Express

FREIGHT SHAKER – Freightliner

FROG - ABF Freight

J.B. - J.B.Hunt

K.W. – Kentworth

MOVIE STAR - M.S. Carriers

PETE – Peterbuilt

PUMPKIN - Snider

WALLY WORLD – Walmart

WERNIE - Werner Transportation

Into the Woods

You never know where your load is going to take you.

Once, I called in for a load and they asked if I wanted one in Georgia. It would be a load of used 7-up bottles and I was to take them to a plant back in the woods.

I said yes, and sure enough it was a load of used bottles. They even had residue of pop still in them. Once I was loaded, I was off to deliver them. It was beautiful in the country. But, going into the backwoods, I started worrying that I had missed a turnoff. It did not look like I would find a plant for this load out here in the wilds!

Finally, I could not believe it! Here was this huge plant out in the boondocks. Well, guess what they made? Carpet and clothing from polypropylene. After they sterilize and melt down the plastic, they make the most beautiful thread. They even gave me a tour of the plant.

I always enjoyed this type of load.

Call Your Daughter ASAP

Driving down the interstate at about 8 p.m. I got a message on my computer sent from my company. Call Jan ASAP. Jan was my oldest daughter.

Now this was a time when computers were just coming of age. We didn't have cell phones yet, but my company was able to contact me with a computer they had installed in the cab.

I was on I-10 going west and in between rest areas. My mind was racing. What could it be? My son? My other daughter? My grandchildren, my parents? At the first rest area there was no phone. I had to wait for a truck stop. I raced to the phone and called Jan.

M: What is wrong, Honey?"

(My daughter was a labor and delivery nurse).

J: Oh! MOM, I just delivered my first baby and I was so excited I couldn't sleep and had to call and tell you."

M: Super, Baby, I am very proud of you! But don't tell my Company ASAP next time.

This is an event in my life I will never forget.

Load from Hell

I started driving in 1983. In 1984 the company sent me up the coast of California for a soap load. This load was to be pre-loaded and ready for pick-up. It sounded like a great load. It was going to Boston for a Friday a.m. delivery. Super! I would have time to empty the trailer and get reloaded for a run over the week-end. I hurried up, found my load ... 900 50-lb boxes for a total of 45,000 lbs. I dropped my empty trailer, and hooked up.

The trip took a bit longer than planned. This was a 50-foot loaded trailer for a total of 79,000 lbs. Pulling up the mountains was going to take some time because my company only had cab-over trucks with minimum power.
After finally arriving in Boston in the early a.m. and squeezing around the small streets and corners, I found the plant. Setting the brake and the flashers, off I went to find the receivers office.

Here are your bills of lading for the load from California.

R: OK put it in dock #3.

M: Do you want to break the seal.

R: Have the dock driver do it.

I pulled into the yard and found dock #3. Once I had backed into the dock and the dock man had cut the seal, he waved to me to come up on the dock. OK. I hopped up on the dock and looked into the trailer. The load was beautiful - 900 boxes on pallets and shrink-wrapped.

The warehouse driver was sitting on a fork lift and wanted this perfect load changed.

D: Lady I don't cross the yellow line on the dock. Drag empty pallets into the trailer and reload 4 high and use the pallet jack to drag them to the tail gate of the trailer.

I suppose if I had offered him some moula, he would have had this load in the warehouse in a jiffy. Well, I guess I am stubborn, and I wasn't about to give in.

So, I unloaded those 900 50-lb boxes, in a trailer that was at least 110 degrees in the middle of summer. For thanks I got a ruptured disc and ended up in the hospital once I got back home.

Sometimes it doesn't pay to be stubborn. But, it was the principle of it.

On the Road

Loading empty stick trailer on the back of a tractor

Stick loader at the sawmill

Loading a truck with sawdust

Emptying the truck at the sawmill

On the Road

Used cardboard going to be recycled

Inside a paper plant

Rolls of paper loaded in the trailer

Trucks covoying in Amarillo, Texas, hoping to "cheat" the ice. More ice photos on pages 30, 56 and 57.

On the Road

The Good Guys

Breaker, Breaker. Anyone with a copy. The bear has me at the Big Road. He's looking for a bobtail that was involved in a 10-33 with a 4-wheeler coming our of the pickle park.

The Good Guys

The Good Guys

Scraaawww..!!
Breaker, Breaker, in the chicken hauler. We've got a crotch rocket coming up on our donkey and he's running like a cowboy. Hope the bears have got their ears on!

The Good Guys

Breaker, breaker, in the blue Freight Shaker, by the time you pass the chicken coops a city kitty is gonna be on your donkey! He's giving me a safety award now!

Now remember, when that parking lot is full, take off for Mexico, but hurry back. There's another concert in Alameda next week!

How far to the Rock, Officer?

Dedication

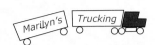

This book is dedicated to my grandkids:
Michael, Kristen, Joseph, Danielle and Meghan.
You were my inspiration.

I would also like to express my grateful
appreciation to a friend of 30 years, Bill Turner,
"Chips," whose drawings of the *Good Guys* bring
color and humor to these pages.

Changing the Rules

Things are Getting Better

Back in the early 80s to get into the trucking industry, you had to start with a company that was considered to be on the low end of quality companies. You had to drive for 1 to 2 years with no accidents, tickets, or late loads. And you had to be able to handle your rig on ice and snow, and in all types of weather. Furthermore, driving for a low-end quality company, you had:

1.   Cheaper equipment.
2.   Lots of layovers.
3.   Weeks away from home.
4.   Low pay.
5.   Lots of fingerprint loads.
6.   Lots of heavy loads.
7.   Equipment needing repair.

In 1999 the NTSB (National Transportation Safety Board), the Government, the ATA (American Trucking Association), and the trucking industry started hearings regarding the upgrading of the trucking industry's rules and regulations.

The Hours of Service rule was over 60 years old and needed to be reviewed. Also in need of review were the rules for shippers and receivers: how they were making drivers load and unload and then drive, causing fatigue; how they were not holding to scheduled appointments unless you drove for a union company. With Homeland Security getting involved, changes were made.

Deregulation of the trucking industry changed the whole industry, and these changes were welcomed by the drivers.

1.   If you haul hazmat products, you are required to go through a background check. People who have spent time in prison cannot haul hazmat.

2.   You must have a physical every year if you have high blood pressure or diabetes.

3.   Otherwise you must have a physical every 2 years.

4.   There is spot testing for drugs

Help Promote **Wreck**Less Driving.
Don't hang out in the **NO-ZONE**

In a program organized by the American Trucking Association Marilyn puller a trailer whose painted sides illustrated how to drive safely around big rigs.

Driver's Test

How much do you know about the trucking industry?

1. How many hours can a driver drive per week?

2. How often do drivers have to take a physical?

3. How much weight can the drivers on the tractor haul while hooked to a trailer?

4. How much weight can rest on the tandems (pivots over rear wheels) of the trailer?

5. What is the total maximum weight for the tractor and trailer together?

6. What lanes can a semi-tractor-trailer drive in?

7. How often do drivers have to renew their license?

8. How often does a driver have to renew his hazmat endorsement

9. What kind of clearance do you need to haul hazmat materials?

10. What do you inspect on the tractor and trailer?

11. What kind of license is required for truck drivers?

12. What are placards?

continued on page 71

Breaker, Breaker. Mrs. C here to the the covered wagon on my donkey. If you have your ears on, stand on it and you can keep rollin' at the chicken coop. Looks like it's feedin' time.

The Good Guys

A bottom dumper

continued from page 68

13. How much fuel tax does each truck on the road pay, and what are these taxes used for?

14. How much road tax do trucks pay?

15. What is a log book?

16. How do you say log book in CB Lingo?

17. What is the maximum height of tractor and trailer?

18. What is the gross vehicle weight?

19. What are the allowable lengths of trailers?

20. What is a bobtail?

21. What exactly is a bottom dumper? *See the picture on the left.*

answers on page 72

Driver's Test

continued from page 71

Driver's Test Answer Key

1. *How many hours can a driver drive per week?* 70 hours in 8 days.

2. *How often do drivers have to take a physical?* Every 2 years, unless they have high blood pressure or medical problems.

3. *How much weight can the drivers on the tractor haul while hooked to a trailer?* 34.000 lbs

4. *How much weight can rest on the tandems (pivots over rear wheels) of the trailer?* 34,000 lbs

5. *What is the total maximum weight for the tractor and trailer together?* 80,000 lbs

6. *What lanes can a semi-tractor-trailer drive in?* The two right lanes only (in California). This differs in some states.

7. *How often do drivers have to renew their license?* With a good record, every 5 yrs.

8. *How often does a driver have to renew his hazmat endorsement?* Every 3 yrs, some every 5 yrs.

9. *What kind of clearance do you need to haul hazmat materials?* Drivers have to have a Transportation Security Clearance from Homeland Security.

10. *What do you inspect on the tractor and trailer?* Wheels, tires, rims, springs, spring hangers, shackles, u-bolts, shocks, mirrors, windshield wipers, turn signals, lights, fuel tanks, glad hands (coupling devices used to connect the air lines from the truck to the tractor), kingpins, landing gear dollies, rear doors and air hoses under the trailer.

continued on page 74

Okay, a driver at the chicken coop said there was a big gator at the mile marker. So I stopped to kick it off the asphalt ... and it really was a gator !!!

Driver's Test

continued from page 72

11. *What kind of license is required for truck drivers?* A commercial license ? (C.D.L.)

12. *What are placards?* Signs identifing hazmat loads, and what is in the trailer.

13. *How much fuel tax does each truck on the road pay, and what are these taxes used for?* $7 to $10,000 every year for road improvements.

14. *How much road tax do trucks pay?* Average $8 to $10,000 per year.

15. *What is a log book?* All drivers who operate a commercial motor vehicle are required to keep a daily log. Logs are to be kept current and a copy of each log for the past 7 days must be in their possession while on duty.

16. *How do you say log book in CB Lingo?* Comic book.

17. *What is the maximum height of tractor and trailer?* 13 feet 6 inches.

18. *What is the gross vehicle weight?* 80,000 lbs.

19. *What are the allowable lengths of trailers?* Standard: 45' to 53' standard. Doubles: 45' to 48' (legal in 18 states). Triples: 26 to 29'. Pups legal in 17 states. Triples are restricted to major highways and toll roads.

20. *What is a bobtail?* A tractor with no trailer.

21. *What exactly is a bottom dumper?* See the picture on page 71. It is a trailer that loads from the top and unloads from the bottom.

The Good Guys

Breaker, Breaker. There's a skate board on its side going in to Music City and the hook is in the fast lane. You better slow poke that thermos bottle. There are plain wrappers, full growns, and county mounties coming and going. Come on back.

States Quiz

Answer Key
from page 45

BIG SKY	MONTANA
BIKINI	FLORIDA
BUCKEYE	OHIO
GARDEN STATE	NEW JERSEY
GRANITE STATE	NEW HAMPSHIRE
GREEN MOUNTAIN STATE	VERMONT
HILLBILITY	WEST VIRGINIA
HOG COUNTRY	ARKANSAS
KEY STONE	PENNSYLVANIA
LEFT COAST	CALIFORNIA
MISERY	MISSOURI
OAKIE	OKLAHOMA
STICKER PATCH	ARIZONA
TAR HILL	NORTH CAROLINA
UT	UTAH

Credits

Book Design
Virginia Lawrence

Cartoons
Bill Turner (Chips)

Photos and Texts
Marilyn Cochrane Hoffman

Back Cover
*Photography by Carolyn
Menifee, CA*